Context Effects on Embodied Representation of Language Concepts

Context Effects on Embodied Representation of Language Concepts

Jie Yang
Brain Circuits Laboratory,
Department of Neurology,
University of California,
Irvine, CA, USA

ELSEVIER

AMSTERDAM • BOSTON • HEIDELBERG • LONDON
NEW YORK • OXFORD • PARIS • SAN DIEGO
SAN FRANCISCO • SINGAPORE • SYDNEY • TOKYO
Academic Press is an imprint of Elsevier

Academic Press is an imprint of Elsevier
The Boulevard, Langford Lane, Kidlington, Oxford, OX5 1GB, UK
225 Wyman Street, Waltham, MA 02451, USA

First published 2013

Copyright © 2013 Elsevier Inc. All rights reserved.

No part of this publication may be reproduced or transmitted in any form or by any means, electronic or mechanical, including photocopying, recording, or any information storage and retrieval system, without permission in writing from the publisher. Details on how to seek permission, further information about the Publisher's permissions policies and our arrangement with organizations such as the Copyright Clearance Center and the Copyright Licensing Agency, can be found at our website: www.elsevier.com/permissions

This book and the individual contributions contained in it are protected under copyright by the Publisher (other than as may be noted herein).

Notices
Knowledge and best practice in this field are constantly changing. As new research and experience broaden our understanding, changes in research methods, professional practices, or medical treatment may become necessary.

Practitioners and researchers must always rely on their own experience and knowledge in evaluating and using any information, methods, compounds, or experiments described herein. In using such information or methods they should be mindful of their own safety and the safety of others, including parties for whom they have a professional responsibility.

To the fullest extent of the law, neither the Publisher nor the authors, contributors, or editors, assume any liability for any injury and/or damage to persons or property as a matter of products liability, negligence or otherwise, or from any use or operation of any methods, products, instructions, or ideas contained in the material herein.

British Library Cataloguing in Publication Data
A catalogue record for this book is available from the British Library

Library of Congress Cataloging-in-Publication Data
A catalog record for this book is available from the Library of Congress

ISBN: 978-0-12-407816-1

For information on all Academic Press publications
visit our website at store.elsevier.com

This book has been manufactured using Print On Demand technology. Each copy is produced to order and is limited to black ink. The online version of this book will show color figures where appropriate.

Transferred to Digital Printing in 2013

CONTENTS

Context Effects on Embodied Representation of Language Concepts 1
1.1 Theories About Automatic Embodied Representation 2
1.2 Theories About Context-Dependent Embodied Representation 3
1.3 Evidence for Automatic Embodied Representation 5
1.4 EEG and MEG Evidences 5
1.5 fMRI Evidence 6
1.6 Evidence for Context-Dependent Embodied Representation 8
1.7 Discussion 14
1.8 Conclusion 19
References 20

Context Effects on Embodied Representation of Language Concepts

Conceptual knowledge is abstract information representing different categories in the world. It is fundamental for various cognitive functions, such as object recognition, language comprehension and production, knowledge acquisition, decision making, and so on.

Nevertheless, how conceptual knowledge is represented and processed in the human brain is still unknown. Although amodal theories assume that concepts resides in a modular semantic system separate from modality-specific systems for perception and action (Fodor, 1975; Pylyshyn, 1984; Smith & Medin, 1981; Tulving, 1972), increased evidence from behavioral, electroencephalographic (EEG)/magnetoencephalographic (MEG), functional magnetic resonance imaging (fMRI), and transcranial magnetic stimulation (TMS) studies indicate that representation of conceptual knowledge is grounded in modality-specific systems, and brain regions underpin perception and action are also involved in conceptual processing. These findings suggest that representation of concepts is grounded in the sensory–motor system.

One debate about the embodied representation is whether it is stable, that is, whether it is independent of linguistic or extra-linguistic context. Although conceptual knowledge is traditionally assumed to be stable and retrieved from memory in a situational invariant fashion, many researchers have claimed that the embodied representation is context dependent and flexible (Barsalou, 2003; Kiefer, 2005; Yeh & Barsalou, 2006) given the fact that different contexts can emphasize different semantic features in the concepts.

This chapter reviewed theories about the automaticity or contextual flexibility of embodied representation and the evidence supporting of these theories. Subsequently, three issues were raised about the current evidence: first, whether the flexibility happens in the presemantic stages (i.e., the stages where the sensory–motor system makes functional contributions to semantic processing) are still in controversy. Second, specific influences from different contexts on embodied representation still need to be distinguished. Third, influences from metalinguistic tasks used in the current studies need to be investigated and clarified.

1.1 THEORIES ABOUT AUTOMATIC EMBODIED REPRESENTATION

So far several theories have claimed the automaticity of embodied representation. Pulvermüller (1999) proposed that neurons in different cortical areas active at the same time can form cell assemblies that are strongly connected. The distribution of the cell assemblies in the brain reflects how neurons are activated during learning. Words in different categories all include a left lateralized perisylvian part representing phonological word form, and neurons outside the perisylvian areas are added to assembly if words refer to actions and perceptions. For action words, a perisylvian assembly is linked to neurons in motor, premotor, and prefrontal cortices related to motor program. For object words, a perisylvian assembly and neurons in visual cortices are linked to represent perception meanings.

Pulvermüller (2001) mentioned that during word acquisition, in neurons representing word forms and neurons representing stimuli, the words referred to are repeatedly active at the same time. Thus, they tend to be associated and activity in one can facilitate activity in the other. Because word-form processing can be fast and automatic (Krause et al., 1998), neurons related to motor or perception processes referred to by words can be automatically and invariably activated when action or perception words are encountered.

Pulvermüller (2005) discussed the neural mechanism of comprehending action-related words. One important issue is whether the comprehension of the action words can specifically, rapidly, and automatically activate the motor system in a somatotopic manner. The author claimed a semantic somatotopy model. According to the model, the perception of spoken and written action words can activate brain regions responsible for action planning and execution in a category-specific somatotopic fashion. The internal connections of the neuronal assemblies are achieved through fast-conducting axons, and thus the spread activation from word-form perception areas to the sensorimotor areas related to the referred meaning is rapid and early. Furthermore, this fast activation is automatic and does not require people pay attention to the language stimuli.

1.2 THEORIES ABOUT CONTEXT-DEPENDENT EMBODIED REPRESENTATION

Theories about flexible embodied representation assume that involvement of the sensory–motor system in conceptual representation is context dependent, and can be modified by linguistic or extra-linguistic factors.

Simmons, Hamann, Harenski, Hu, and Barsalou (2008) proposed that language comprehension relies on both the language and the situated simulation (LASS) system. The language system is responsible for processing word-form information, and the situated stimulation system is responsible for representing conceptual knowledge. When a word is presented, both systems are activated but the language system peaks first. After the word-form information is recognized by the language system, the word's representation begins to activate simulations contributing to the word's meaning. Although the model assumes that these simulations are often activated automatically and quickly, it also claims that different task demands can cause different mixtures of LASS: when word-form information is sufficient to support task performance, word processing will mostly rely on the language system and little on the situated simulation system; when word-form information alone cannot sufficiently support task performance (e.g., the task requires semantic judgment), the situated simulation system will be activated to provide conceptual information. Task demand therefore can modulate situated simulation. The LASS theory comes from the Dual Code theory (Paivio, 1971, 1986) that claims the presence of linguistic and perceptual representations in many areas of cognition.

Rüschemeyer, Lindemann, van Elk, and Bekkering (2008) claimed that while unspecific, motor resonance (i.e., the general awareness that a word has an action association) can be highly automatic. Action context can modulate the activation of sensory–motor features of an object and generate a strategic context-specific processing level. If the representation of an object is associated with multiple action possibilities, then one's action intention can determine whether an action representation should be activated. For example, when we want to read a newspaper, the features "light (easy to hold)" "full of words," and "multiple pages" of a newspaper can be highly activated; when we want to cover something with a newspaper, the features "wide," "flat," and "nontransparent" can be highly activated. Thus, selection of alternative action goals can cause selective activation of semantic information that is consistent with one's action intention.

Yeh and Barsalou (2006) suggested that background situations are fundamental to cognition. A situation is "a region of perceived space that surrounds a focal entity over some temporal duration, perceived from the subjective perspective of an agent." A situation can contain various entities, events, and mental states. Because in a certain situation, specific entities and events tend to occur, the cognitive system focuses on the knowledge and skills relevant in the current situation and simplifies many tasks. Thus, situation can facilitate processing. In language comprehension, situations can place an important constrain on concepts: if sensory–motor simulation plays an important role in conceptual representation and processing (Barsalou, 1999, 2008), then the simulation is mainly about the situation where the referred perception or action occurs. This is because situations are intrinsic parts of perceptual experiences. Background situations constrain conceptual processing in many tasks, such as lexical decision, property verification, categorization, recognition, and so on.

In the review about conceptual representation, Kiefer and Pulvermüller (2012) claimed that word meanings are constituted of dynamically-recruited features depending on context. Nondominant semantic features of a concept need a contextual support to become activated, while the dominant semantic features do not require such a support (Barsalou, 1982). Thus, the activity of semantic features contributing to a concept can be regarded as a function of the dominance and of the contextual constrains. At a neural level, conceptual flexibility can be modeled as cell assemblies that constrained both by the established connections between neurons and by the influences of the situation that prime different sets of neurons (Hoenig, Sim, Bochev, Herrnberger, and Kiefer, 2008; Kiefer, 2005; Pulvermüller, 1999). This suggests that conceptual representations and their neurobiological underpinnings should be viewed as context dependent.

1.3 EVIDENCE FOR AUTOMATIC EMBODIED REPRESENTATION
1.3.1 Behavioral Evidence
To test whether the involvement of sensory–motor regions during semantic processing is automatic, researchers examined whether action affordances can be activated by language stimuli when the affordance is only implicitly represented. In Glover, Rosenbaum, Graham, and Dixon (2004), participants read words representing graspable objects that are large (e.g., *apple*) or small (e.g., *grape*). The words implicitly represent the grasping actions associated with the objects. Participants then grasped a wooden block. The authors found an interference effect in the early portions of the grasping performance: reading a word about a large object led to a larger grip aperture (i.e., larger separation between the thumb and the index finger) than reading a word about a small object. The results suggest that action affordances can be activated implicitly and support the view that the involvement of sensory–motor system during semantic processing is automatic.

In social cognition field, numerous behavioral studies have found strong associations between metaphorically related physical and psychological concepts. Examples include physical warmth elicits feelings of social warmth (Bargh & Shalev, 2012; Williams & Bargh, 2008), physical heaviness activates feelings of seriousness, and physical sensations of surface hardness prime more abstract notions of difficulty (Ackerman, Nocera, & Bargh, 2010). These results suggest that activation automatically spreads from concepts about physical experiences to concepts about psychological experiences (for a review, see Bargh, Schwader, Hailey, Dyer, & Boothby, 2012).

1.4 EEG AND MEG EVIDENCES
If the involvement of sensory–motor regions is automatic, then activity on these regions should be observed irrespective of subject's attention. The mismatch negativity (MMN) is a neurophysiological brain response recorded in EEG and MEG, and it can be elicited by both attended and unattended stimuli. Previous studies have shown that MMN size and topography can reflect the activation of memory traces for language elements even under attentional withdrawal. For example, Shtyrov, Hauk and Pulvermüller (2004) used MMN to investigate the representation of action-related words in human brain. Participants listened to action-related words and their brain responses were

recorded by a high-density EEG system. A nonattend odd-ball protocol was used: participants watched a silent video film of their own choice. The same words were presented as standard stimuli and deviant stimuli in different sessions to avoid the phonetic−acoustic differences. The results showed that words related to hand actions elicited a more widespread lateral distribution, whereas words related to leg actions had a more focal dorsal negativity. This result pattern was confirmed by distributed source analysis, and this suggests that distributed neuronal assemblies can function as category-specific memory traces for words. Moreover, the results showed that the sensory−motor system can be involved independent of attention. Pulvermüller, Shtyrov, and Ilmoniemi (2005) tested whether there is fast spreading of neuronal activity from language areas to specific sensory−motor areas during action words processing. Participants were presented with words related to face or leg actions while distracted by a silent movie. Their brain responses were recorded with high-density MEG. The objective source localization method revealed activations in the superior temporal areas at 130 ms after stimulus onset and activations in the inferior frontocentral areas at 142−146 ms. Furthermore, the face words showed stronger effects in the inferior frontocentral areas than the leg words, while the leg words showed stronger effects in the superior central cites. The action ratings about the word stimuli were correlated with the local source strengths in the frontocentral cortex. These results indicate that meaning access of action words can be early, fast, and automatic, independent of participants' attention.

1.5 fMRI EVIDENCE

Hauk, Johnsrude, and Pulvermüller (2004) used a passive reading task to investigate the functional anatomy of action verb comprehension. Participants read verbs referring to face, arm, or leg actions (e.g., *lick*, *pick*, *kick*) without moving their hands, head, and bodies. After the language task, participants were asked to move their left or right foot, left or right index finger, and tongue to identify motor areas responsible for hand, foot, and face movements. Compared to baseline condition (viewing hash marks), all three types of verbs showed activations in the left inferior temporal gyrus (ITG) and left inferior frontal gyrus (IFG). Face words specifically activated ventral premotor cortex, arm words elicited activity dorsal to the effect of fact words in the premotor cortex, and leg words produced activity in the dorsal areas in midline precentral and postcentral gyri. These activations partially overlapped with the effects elicited by real movements and the activation pattern is consistent with a somatotopic organization.

If the motor region involvement during the meaning access of action words is automatic, then activation of motor areas should be found both when action words are presented in isolation and when they occur in sentential contexts. In Aziz-Zadeh, Wilson, Rizzolatti, and Iacoboni (2006), participants passively read literal phrases about different body actions (e.g., *biting the peach, grasping the scissors,* and *pressing the car brake*) and watched videos of mouth, hand, or foot actions. Region of interest (ROI) analysis based on action observation showed a clear congruence between visually presented actions and action described by language stimuli: in the left premotor cortex, hand action phrases showed stronger activity than mouth and foot action phrases in the hand area, while in the foot action phrases showed stronger activity than mouth and hand action phrases.

Tettamanti et al. (2005) found that passively listening to sentences describing actions performed by mouth, hand, and leg activated a left fronto–parieto–temporal network. Additionally, ROI analysis based on body-part-specific effects showed that the sentences about leg motions had the highest signal change in the dorsal area of premotor cortex, the sentences about hand motions had the highest signal change in the ventral part to this effect, and the sentences about mouth motions had the highest signal change in the ventral part to the effects of hand and leg sentences.

The somatotopic activation pattern was also found in passively listening to complicated action-related sentences. In Raposo, Moss, Stamatakis, and Tyler (2009), participants listened to single words related to arm and leg actions. After that, participants moved their left or right index finger and left or right foot to do a movement localizer task. ROI analysis based on the localizer task showed that in the motor area activated by finger movement, arm words indicated higher effect size than that of leg words, while in the motor area activated by leg movement, leg words indicated higher effect size than that of arm words. In another experiment, participants listened to long sentences related to arm or leg actions (e.g., *the fruit cake was the last one so Claire grabbed it*). The activations in motor regions were still significant although to a less extent compare to those in the isolated verb condition.

Boulenger, Hauk, and Pulvermüller (2009) found that when action verbs were presented in figurative contexts, such as idioms, the motor effects still could be observed even though the action meaning of the verbs was not required. In the study, participants read literal sentences and idioms containing arm- or leg-related action verbs (e.g., *He grasped the object* or *He grasped the idea*). The results showed that somatotopic activations along the motor strip in the premotor and the primary motor cortex were elicited by both literal and idiomatic sentences. Additionally, the semantic somatotopy was most pronounced after sentence ending. Similarly, Lacey, Stilla, and Sathian (2012) found that when participants listened to sentences containing textural metaphors (e.g., *She had a rough day*), texture-selective somatosensory area in the parietal operculum was activated compared to control sentences (e.g., *She had a bad day*). These findings suggest that the semantic representation of sentence-level meaning is grounded in the sensory–motor system and the involvement of sensory–motor areas is automatic, independent of language context (but see Aziz-Zadeh et al., 2006 and Raposo et al., 2009).

To summarize, these findings indicate that activations in motor areas can be early, fast, and automatic, independent of context and participants' attention.

1.6 EVIDENCE FOR CONTEXT-DEPENDENT EMBODIED REPRESENTATION

1.6.1 Behavioral Evidence

Solomon and Barsalou (2004) used a property verification task to test whether people represent concepts with perceptual simulations. In each trial, participants saw a word describing an object concept (e.g., *CAT*) which was followed by a word describing a property (e.g., *fur*), and they decided whether the property was true for the object. The participants were divided into two groups. One was imagery group that was explicitly asked to use the simulation strategy for property verification. The other was neutral group that received no explicit instructions for verifying properties. Sometimes the property and the object were completely unassociated with each other (e.g., *PLIERS-river*). Sometimes although the property was not true for the object, they were highly associated (e.g., *OTTER-river*). The manipulation of the false trial modulated participants' strategy for doing the judgment. For the false trials that were unassociated, participants could use associativeness information to make decisions and did not have to activate perceptual simulations. When the false trials were highly associated, however, participants could not rely on the associativeness information, and they had to activate perceptual simulation to access information about the conceptual relations between objects and properties. This prediction was confirmed by the results: the neural group showed similar result patterns to that of the imagery group only when the false trials were highly associated. This suggests that simulation during conceptual processing can be influenced by task demand.

Sato, Mengarelli, Riggio, Gallese, and Buccino (2008) investigated how motor system modulates action language processing. In one experiment, participants processed verbs about hand and foot actions and perform a go/no-go semantic judgment task (whether the presented verb describes a concrete action). The results showed that responses on hand action verbs were slower than responses on foot action verbs. However, such a difference was not observed when participants performed a lexical-decision task. This finding indicates that motor system can modulate language comprehension, but this modulation can be influenced by the task demand.

van Dam, Rüschemeyer, Lindemann, and Bekkering (2010) investigated whether a word always activates a specific motor feature or whether the activation of a motor feature depends on the context in which a word is presented. In the study, participants prepared a movement and performed a lexical-decision task on object words. The object words were preceded by a prime word which provided a context emphasizing either a dominant action feature (*thirst—cup*) or a non-dominant action feature (*sink—cup*). Furthermore, the direction of the participant's movement and the motor program associated with the word's referent could be corresponded or not (action congruent vs action incongruent). The results showed that congruency influenced lexical decision: participants gave faster responses when the functional use of the word's referent was congruent with the prepared movement. Furthermore, this congruency effect was only significant when the dominant action feature of words was emphasized by the semantic context. The results suggest that conceptual processing is context dependent and the usage of motor feature is flexible.

Rüschemeyer, Lindemann, van Rooij, van Dam, and Bekkering (2010) showed that action goals can affect the semantic processing of words. Participants performed either intentional or passive actions and while doing a lexical-decision task on words describing manipulable or unmanipulable objects. The authors found that performing intentional actions could actively affect the lexical decision of words denoting manipulable objects. But such effect was not observed when participants performed passive motor tasks. The results demonstrate a selectivity effect of action execution on word comprehension. Performing intentional actions and semantic processing of action-related words can engage common parts of the motor system.

1.6.2 EEG and MEG Evidence

van Elk, van Schie, Zwaan, and Bekkering (2010) tested whether the language-induced motor activation primarily reflects the retrieval of semantic information. Participants read sentences about human actions (e.g., *the woman is swimming in the water*) and animal actions (e.g., *the duck is swimming in the pond*) and performed a word–sentence association judgment. The EEG results showed a desynchronization in the mu- and beta-frequency bands localized on the motor and the premotor areas, which reflected an early activation (preceded classical measures of semantic integration, the N400 component) of motor-related areas during action sentence processing. Furthermore, the motor activation effect was modulated by sentential context: animal contexts elicited stronger effects than human contexts. This finding suggests that the motor system is involved in language processing at an early stage and can be modulated by contextual information. However, it is surprising to see animal action sentences showed stronger effects as simulating human actions should be easier than simulating animal actions.

Hoenig, Sim, Bochev, Herrnberger, and Kiefer (2008) combined fMRI and EEG techniques to test whether conceptual representation can be modulated by experimental situation (i.e., task demand). In the study, participants performed a semantic attribute verification task that requires them to decide whether a verbal attribute probe referring to action or visual features was semantically consistent with the successively presented words about objects. The described objects can be either artifactual (e.g., *knife*) or natural (e.g., *orange*). In the semantic representation of artifactual objects, the action feature is dominant, while in natural objects, the visual feature is dominant. The event-related potential (ERP) results revealed that the interaction effect between task demand and object category occurred as early as 116 ms after stimulus onset. The fMRI results showed that areas in the left IFG, superior parietal gyrus (SPG), ITG, and middle temporal gyrus (MTG) have strong interaction: In both types of objects, the nondominant semantic feature was highly activated by task demand. This finding indicates that the access to the conceptual features is not after effects based on comprehension. The interaction effects suggest that conceptual representation can be situational dependent.

Several studies found that action goals can modulate semantic processing of words. For example, van Elk, van Schie, and Bekkering (2008) revealed that lexical–semantic processing can be influenced by action goals. In that study, participants prepared meaningful or meaningless actions with objects, and then performed a semantic categorization judgment on a word (i.e., decide whether the word describes a body part or an animal). The presented words can be either congruent or incongruent with the goal of the prepared action. The results showed that when the action goals were meaningful, a larger N400 was elicited for incongruent words compared to congruent words. However, such an effect was not observed when the action goals were meaningless. This finding suggests that semantic information can be activated during preparing meaningful actions, and thus the subsequent lexical–semantic processing is influenced.

1.6.3 TMS Evidence

In Papeo, Vallesi, Isaja, and Rumiati (2009), TMS was applied at 170, 350, and 500 ms poststimulus onset during a semantic judgment task (i.e., to decide whether the presented word is action related) and a syllabic judgment task (i.e., to decide the number of syllables in each word) to identify when the enhancement of M1-activity happens during word comprehension. The results showed that only when TMS was applied at 500 ms poststimulus, the M1-activity in the action verbs was different from that in the nonaction verbs. Additionally, the M1-activity was increased in the semantic task but decreased in the syllabic task. This finding suggests that M1 was involved in action language processing in a postconceptual processing and this late involvement is modulated by task demand.

1.6.4 fMRI Evidence

Several studies have found that language context can modulate the involvement of the sensory–motor system. For instance, Rüschemeyer,

Brass, and Friederici (2007) investigated the neural correlates of processing concrete and abstract verbs. Two types of verbs were used: simple and morphologically complex verbs. Simple verbs like *greifen* (*to grasp*) express concrete meanings, while verbs like *denken* (*to think*) express abstract meanings. The morphologically complex verbs express abstract meanings and include stems with motor vs. abstract meanings (e.g., *begreifen, to comprehend*, in which the *greifen* means *to grasp*; *bedenken, to consider*, in which *denken* means *to think*). The results showed that while processing concrete simple verbs elicited higher activations in the left central sulcus, precentral gyrus, bilateral postcentral gyrus, and right parietal operculum, processing complex verbs with motor stems showed no differences in the motor system compared to verbs with abstract stems. The main differences between the two types of complex verbs were located in the right posterior MTG and the left cerebellum. The results suggest that abstract verb meanings are not necessarily grounded in a full representation of its component part. It also suggests that the motor responses are context dependent, rather than automatic and invariable.

Tettamanti et al. (2008) showed that passively listening to action-related sentences activated the left action-representation system. This effect was significantly reduced when the polarity of the sentences was negative compared to the effect when the polarity of the sentences was positive. Furthermore, effective connectivity analysis showed weaker functional integration effects in the negative action-related sentences than in the affirmative sentences. These results indicate that sentential context can modulate the involvement of sensory–motor system during action language processing.

Raposo et al. (2009) found that when action verbs appeared in isolation or literal contexts, the somatotopic pattern of activations in the motor system was observable. However, when the action verbs were presented in idiomatic contexts (e.g., *grab an idea*) in which the literal meaning was not required, no activation was found in motor and premotor cortices. Similarly, Aziz-Zadeh et al. (2006) found somatotopic activity in the premotor cortex for literal stimuli, but there was no significant motor activation for idiomatic phrases (e.g., *kicking of the year*). The results again suggest that the involvement of motor system in action language comprehension is context dependent and flexible. However, one possible interpretation in Aziz-Zadeh et al. (2006) is that when the idiomatic phrases were repeated many times, the figurative meaning irrelevant to the original meaning of the action verbs became more and more dominant while the literal meaning became less and less important. This could hinder the activation of the motor system and thus no somatotopic activation along the premotor cortex was found.

Different sensory–motor features can trigger different activity in sensory–motor regions during semantic processing. In visual domain, evidence shows that the richness of visual information associated with a word can modulate the activity in visual areas during word comprehension (Gauthier, Anderson, Tarr, Skudlarski, & Gore, 1997). Words describing subordinate level members of a semantic category (e.g., *pelican*, a member of the category "bird") can show stronger activations in primary visual cortex than those describing basic level members did (e.g., *bird*). This is because the subordinate level members contain more visual features than the basic level members. Recently, researchers investigated whether this is true in the motor domain. In van Dam, Rüschemeyer, and Bekkering (2010), participants read verbs denoting either a general motor program (e.g., *to repair*) or a more specific motor program (e.g., *to hammer*) and performed a go/no-go semantic category judgment. The results showed that bilateral regions involved in action plans and goals (inferior parietal lobule, IPL) were sensitive to the specificity of motor programs. This finding indicates that the concreteness of the action-related semantic feature can modulate the involvement of motor system during action language processing.

Moody and Gennari (2010) examined whether action language stimuli imply different physical efforts can modulate the sensory–motor representation of actions. Stimuli implied more physical effort (e.g., *pushing the piano*) and less physical effort (e.g., *pushing the chair*) were presented and participants answered comprehension questions about them (19% of trials). The results showed that activation in the premotor region was sensitive to the degree of effort described by the language stimuli.

Finally, task demand can affect how sensory–motor regions are involved. Kan, Barsalou, Solomon, Minor, and Thompson-Schill (2003) used fMRI to examine the activity in visual cortex when participants performed a property verification task on associated and unassociated false trials. The results indicated significant activity in the left fusiform gyrus (FG) when true trials were intermixed with associated false trials but not when true trials were intermixed with unassociated false trials. This result confirms the view that sensory–motor simulation during conceptual processing can be modulated by task demand: When the participants could not use association strategy to perform the task, they used visual simulation to help decide whether a given property was true for an object.

van Dam, van Dongen, Bekkering, and Rüschemeyer (2012) found that the functional integration between the word-form processing areas (e.g., auditory-processing areas) and the perception/action-processing areas was context dependent. In the study, participants listened to words denoting objects with both action and color features (e.g., *boxing glove*, *tennis ball*) and for half of the trials they had to answer questions about the color feature of the objects, while for the other half of the trials, they answered questions about the action feature of the objects. Psychophysiological interaction analysis showed that in action-processing condition the right sensory–motor regions (right precentral gyrus, right SMA, and right IPL) had higher functional connectivity with the bilateral STG. In the color-processing condition, the left cingulated gyrus and the left precuneus indicated more functional connectivity with the bilateral STG. This finding supports the view that conceptual representation is flexible.

Papeo, Rumiati, Cecchetto, and Tomasino (2012) investigated how cognitive context can influence semantic representation of action verbs and state verbs. Participants read hand action verbs or state verbs after mental rotation based on motor strategy (motor context) or visuospatial strategy (nonmotor context). The results showed that compared to reading in nonmotor context, reading in motor context increasingly activated areas in the left primary motor cortex, the bilateral premotor cortex, and the right somatosensory cortex irrespective of the verb category. This indicates that the motor context modulated the sensorimotor responses and might reflect the motor-related strategy during word reading.

1.7 DISCUSSION

If all the evidence was put together, we can see that the activation of the sensory–motor system during language comprehension can be automatic when there is no specific task demand (e.g., passive listening or reading tasks) and even when no attention is paid to the stimuli (e.g., in the odd-ball paradigm in EEG and MEG studies).

Nevertheless, if a specific-processing demand is added, a selective attention to certain type of information (e.g., certain type of semantic feature) is required or the cognitive context (e.g., action goals) changes, then the involvement of sensory–motor system can be context dependent. So far there are some issues need to be addressed regarding the flexibility of embodied representation.

1.7.1 Flexibility in Pre- and Postsemantic Stage During Language Comprehension

Whether the sensory–motor system really makes a functional contribution to semantic representation is still in controversy. While numerous fMRI studies have found somatotopic activation along the motor strip during processing of language related to different body-part actions or activity in the motor cortex during action language comprehension (Aziz-Zadeh et al., 2006; Boulenger et al., 2009; Hauk et al., 2004), the results are inconsistent (Fernandino & Iacoboni, 2010; Postle, McMahon, Ashton, Meredith, & de Zubicaray, 2008; de Zubicaray, Postle, McMahon, Meredith, and Ashton, 2010). Moreover, due to the poor temporal resolution of fMRI technique, it is unclear whether the activation of the sensory–motor cortex in these studies precedes or is after the semantic integration stage (e.g., one index of such stage is the N400 component which appears 400 ms after stimulus onset). If the activation of sensory–motor areas precedes semantic integration, then it is possible that the sensory–motor system functionally contributes to semantic processing. If the activation of sensory–motor areas is after semantic integration, then it is more likely that the sensory–motor system is activated by comprehension and the effect is an after effect such as imagery. Indeed, some of the EEG and MEG studies showed that activity in the motor cortex occurs very early during action language comprehension, earlier than the semantic integration stage (Boulenger et al., 2012; Hoenig et al., 2008; Pulvermüller et al., 2005), while other studies such as TMS studies found that activity in the motor cortex occurs in postsemantic stage (Papeo et al., 2009). If the sensory–motor system is involved in both pre- and postsemantic processing, their mechanisms might be different. Willems, Toni, Hagoort, and Casasanto (2010) discussed the possible differences between implicit motor simulation and explicit motor imagery during action verb comprehension.

If we admit that the involvement of the sensory–motor system is context dependent, it is necessary to clarify whether this flexibility occurs at a presemantic stage or a postsemantic stage, or both. So far the evidence from EEG and TMS findings are not consistent across studies. van Elk et al. (2008) showed that participants' action goals can modulate the lexical−semantic processing and influence the N400 effect. van Elk et al. (2010) found an early activation in the motor and premotor areas indexed by a desynchronization in the mu- and beta-frequency bands, and this early activation was modulated by the sentential contexts about human or animals. Hoenig et al. (2008), using EEG and FMRI, found that activation of visual and action semantic features in words denoting artifactual and natural objects were modulated by task demand in a feature−verification judgment. This interaction effect occurred as early as 116 ms after stimulus onset. These findings suggest that the sensory−motor system can functionally contribute to semantic processing in a flexible manner. However, Papeo et al. (2009) using TMS found that the M1-activity in the action verbs was different from that in the nonaction verbs only when TMS was applied at 500 ms poststimulus. Furthermore, the M1-activity was modulated by the task demand. This finding suggests that flexibility is a feature for the postsemantic sensory−motor effect.

1.7.2 Different Types of Contextual Influences

The previous studies have indicated that various contexts can modulate the activation in sensory−motor areas during semantic processing. One important type of context is task demand, in which participants focus on certain information (e.g., motor semantic features instead of visual semantic features or word-form information instead of semantic information) at one level, and shift their attention to other information at another level. Different task demands modulate participants' selective attention and thus influences the involvement of the sensory−motor system. However, when selective attention shows its influence during semantic processing is still unclear. Regardless of the timing information of the sensory−motor activation, one possibility is that selective attention starts to influence semantic processing before semantic access, that is, from word-form processing, and modulate how word-form processing initiates semantic information. The other possibility is that selective attention shows their influence only at the decision-making stage (i.e., postsemantic stage).

Another important type of context is language context. Previous studies have shown that the activation of sensory−motor regions can be affected by figurative contexts, such as idioms (Raposo et al., 2009) in which the figurative meaning is irrelevant to the original meaning of each element word, or abstract contexts in which an action verb is a word stem, and its meaning is far away from the abstract meaning of the whole word (Rüschemeyer et al., 2007). The influence of this type of context is determined by the degree of conventionalization of the figurative or abstract meaning, that is, whether the figurative or abstract meaning can be accessed directly and independently without activating the literal or original meaning in the sensory–motor domain. If the abstract or figurative meaning is highly conventionalized, then during comprehension it should be activated directly through the recognition of the linguistic information (e.g., word-form information). Thus, during comprehension of idioms such as *kick the bucket*, the original meaning of the elementary verb (e.g., *kick*) should not be activated and thus no motor activation should be found (Raposo et al., 2009). If the abstract or figurative meaning is not conventionalized, then during comprehension it should be activated through the recognition of the literal meaning. This is supported by Desai, Binder, Conant, Mano, and Seigdenberg (2011), that indicated that activity in primary motor and biological motion perception regions was inversely correlated with the familiarity of metaphorical and literal sentences. The conventionalization could happen or be strengthened in a short period, for example, during continuous repetitions of the figurative language stimuli in the experiment. In Aziz-Zadeh et al. (2006), the idiomatic phrases were repeated eight times and the authors failed to find somatotopic activation in the premotor cortex. It is possible that the motor cortex was not involved at all, but it is also possible that the motor activation became less and less when the idiomatic phrases became more and more familiar to participants. Different from selective attention which is easily manipulated by task demand and can play a role at perceptual or decision-making stage during task performance, conventionalization is harder to manipulate and depends more on the language stimuli and participants' language experience. Furthermore, while the modulation of selective attention on activation of certain sensory–motor feature seems to be dichotomous (i.e., processing or not processing a certain type of information), the influence of conventionalization on the activation of certain sensory–motor feature is more likely to be in a continuum because conventionalization of a figurative or abstract meaning is gradually developed.

1.7.3 Influences from Metalinguistic Tasks

A third issue regarding the context-dependent embodied representation is the influence from metalinguistic tasks. Metalinguistic tasks are tasks requiring explicit attention to a certain subcomponent of language processing. This type of tasks can be far away from natural language processing since we normally are not consciously accessed the subcomponent when we use language in daily life. Typical metalinguistic tasks during the research about embodied representation include lexical decision (i.e., decide if a presented item is a real word), semantic association judgment (i.e., decide whether two successive presented stimuli are semantically associated), and feature–verification task (i.e., decide whether a specific feature belongs to an object). These metalinguistic tasks not only require participants focus on a certain part of language processing but also require participants make decisions, and prepare and give motor responses.

Because most studies investigating the flexibility of embodied representation choose action language materials as experimental stimuli and test the activation of the motor system, asking participants to prepare and give motor responses during experiment can be a problem. The motor system is strongly activated by the task demand and thus can contaminate the motor effect elicited by language stimuli. Usually in these studies, a baseline condition requiring motor responses is added as a control. However, this does not help to avoid or solve the problem. The logic of adding such a baseline condition is based on the assumption that the involvement of the motor system in preparing and giving motor responses and the involvement of the motor system during action language processing are independent of each other and addable, and thus during the comparison between the action language condition and the baseline condition, the influence of motor responses can be subtracted. Unfortunately, this assumption can simply be false, and it is highly possible that the involvements of the motor system in preparing and giving motor responses and in action language processing interact with each other. Thus, the motor effect observed from the contrast between action language condition and baseline conditions might not be accurate. Additionally, the decision-making process in these metaanalysis tasks might interact with the processes of action semantic feature and other types of information differently, and this also can influence the motor effects observed in these tasks. Some studies tried to avoid the influence from motor responses by using probe trials. That is, participants only made motor responses on probe trials or filler trials such as pseudowords and gave no responses when experimental stimuli were presented (Boulenger et al., 2009). However, this might not be very helpful as because participants did not know after which trial they should make responses, they had to prepare for motor response all the time.

From this point of view, studies using passive reading or listening task during action language processing seems to be more appropriate. It is interesting that studies using such tasks always find significant motor activations during action language processing. This seems to imply that in daily natural language processing, the involvement of the sensory–motor system during semantic processing is automatic. Nevertheless, these natural tasks cannot prevent participants using imagery strategies, and it is hard to monitor participants' attention during the experiment. Asking participants to perform posttests might be helpful, but it is still hard to control participants' attention during online processing and the language stimuli.

1.8 CONCLUSION

Based on the above evidence and discussions, three trends of future investigations can be expected.

The first trend is about the temporal information of the observed flexibility effect in embodied representation. Whether the flexibility occurs at pre- or postsemantic processing stage depends not only on the nature of the involvement of the sensory–motor system (i.e., making a functional contribution to semantic processing or is caused by comprehension) but also on the nature of contextual influence.

The second trend of the further research is about the influences from different context information. Selective attention, language context, and other contexts, such as cognitive context, have different features and can modulate embodied representation differently. Revealing the specific and the common neural mechanism behind these influences can help us understand the nature of the embodied representation.

The third trend of the future work is to eliminate influences from metalinguistic tasks and clarify that the context-dependent embodied representation is not just elicited by the irrelevant processes required by metalinguistic tasks. Moreover, paradigms that can investigate natural language processing should be developed to investigate the embodied representation of language.

REFERENCES

Ackerman, J. M., Nocera, C. C., & Bargh, J. A. (2010). Incidental haptic sensations influence social judgments and decisions. *Science, 328*, 1712–1715.

Aziz-Zadeh, L., Wilson, S. M., Rizzolatti, G., & Iacoboni, M. (2006). Congruent embodied representations for visually presented actions and linguistic phrases describing actions. *Current Biology, 16*, 1818–1823.

Bargh, J. A., Schwader, K. L., Hailey, S. E., Dyer, R. L., & Boothby, E. J. (2012). Automaticity in social–cognitive processes. *Trends in Cognitive Science, 16*, 593–605. doi:10.1016/j.tics.2012.10.002.

Bargh, J. A., & Shalev, I. (2012). The substitutability of physical and social warmth in daily life. *Emotion, 12*, 154–162.

Barsalou, L. W. (1982). Context-independent and context-dependent information in concepts. *Memory and Cognition, 10*, 82–93.

Barsalou, L. W. (1999). Perceptual symbol systems. *Behavioral and Brain Science, 22*, 577–609.

Barsalou, L. W. (2003). Abstraction in perceptual symbol systems. *Philosophical Transactions of the Royal Society of London, Series B, Biological Sciences, 358*, 1177–1187.

Barsalou, L. W. (2008). Grounded cognition. *Annual Review of Psychology, 59*, 617–645.

Boulenger, V., Hauk, O., & Pulvermüller, F. (2009). Grasping ideas with the motor system: Semantic somatotopy in idiom comprehension. *Cerebral Cortex, 19*, 1905–1914. doi:10.1093/cercor/bhn217.

Boulenger, V., Shtyrov, Y., & Pulvermüller, F. (2012). When do you grasp the idea? MEG evidence for instantaneous idiom understanding. *Neuroimage, 59*, 3502–3513.

Desai, R. H., Binder, J. R., Conant, L. L., Mano, Q. R., & Seidenberg, M. S. (2011). The neural career of sensory–motor metaphors. *Journal of Cognitive Neuroscience, 23*, 2376–2386. doi:10.1162/jocn.2010.21596.

de Zubicaray, G., Postle, N., McMahon, K., Meredith, M., & Ashton, R. (2010). Mirror neurons, the representation of word meaning, and the foot of the third left frontal convolution. *Brain and Language, 112*, 77–84. doi:10.1016/j.bandl.2008.09.011.

Fernandino, L., & Iacoboni, M. (2010). Are cortical motor maps based on body parts or coordinated actions? Implications for embodied semantics. *Brain and Language, 112*, 44–53. doi:10.1016/j.bandl.2009.02.003.

Fodor, J. A. (1975). The languageof thought. Harvard University Press.

Gauthier, I., Anderson, A. W., Tarr, M. J., Skudlarski, P., & Gore, J. C. (1997). Levels of categorization in visual recognition studied using functional magnetic resonance imaging. *Current Biology, 7*, 645–651.

Glover, S., Rosenbaum, D. A., Graham, J., & Dixon, P. (2004). Grasping the meaning of words. *Experimental Brain Research, 154*, 103–108.

Hauk, O., Johnsrude, I., & Pulvermüller, F. (2004). Somatotopic representation of action words in human motor and premotor cortex. *Neuron, 41*, 301–307.

Hoenig, K., Sim, E. J., Bochev, V., Herrnberger, B., & Kiefer, M. (2008). Conceptual flexibility in the human brain: Dynamic recruitment of semantic maps from visual, motor, and motion-related areas. *Journal of Cognitive Neuroscience, 20*, 1799–1814. doi:10.1162/jocn.2008.20123.

Kan, I. P., Barsalou, L. W., Solomon, K. O., Minor, J. K., & Thompson-Schill, S. L. (2003). Role of mental imagery in a property verification task: fMRI evidence for perceptual representations of conceptual knowledge. *Cognitive Neuropsychology, 20*, 525–540. doi:10.1080/02643290244000257.

Kiefer, M. (2005). Repetition priming modulates category-related effects on event-related potentials: Further evidence for multiple cortical semantic systems. *Journal of Cognitive Neuroscience, 17*, 199–211.

Kiefer, M., & Pulvermüller, F. (2012). Conceptual representations in mind and brain: Theoretical developments, current evidence and future directions. *Cortex, 48*, 805–825. doi:10.1016/j.cortex.2011.04.006.

Krause, C. M., Korpilahti, P., Pörn, B., Jäntti, J., & Lang, H. A. (1998). Automatic auditory word perception as measured by 40 Hz EEG responses. *Electroencephalography and Clinical Neurophysiology, 107*, 84–87.

Lacey, S., Stilla, R., & Sathian, K. (2012). Metaphorically feeling: Comprehending textural metaphors activates somatosensory cortex. *Brain and Language, 120*, 416–421. doi:10.1016/j.bandl.2011.12.016.

Moody, C. L., & Gennari, S. P. (2010). Effects of implied physical effort in sensory–motor and pre-frontal cortex during language comprehension. *Neuroimage, 49*, 782–793. doi:10.1016/j.neuroimage.2009.07.065.

Paivio, A. (1971). *Imagery and verbal processes*. New York, NY: Holt, Rinehart, & Winston.

Paivio, A. (1986). *Mental representations: A dual coding approach*. New York, NY: Oxford University Press.

Papeo, L., Rumiati, R. I., Cecchetto, C., & Tomasino, B. (2012). On-line changing of thinking about words: The effect of cognitive context on neural responses to verb reading. *Journal of Cognitive Neuroscience, 24*, 2348–2362. doi:10.1162/jocn_a_00291.

Papeo, L., Vallesi, A., Isaja, A., & Rumiati, R. I. (2009). Effects of TMS on different stages of motor and non-motor verb processing in the primary motor cortex. *PLoS One, 4*, e4508. doi:10.1371/journal.pone.0004508.

Postle, N., McMahon, K. L., Ashton, R., Meredith, M., & de Zubicaray, G. I. (2008). Action word meaning representations in cytoarchitectonically defined primary and premotor cortices. *Neuroimage, 43*, 634–644. doi:10.1016/j.neuroimage.2008.08.006.

Pulvermüller, F. (1999). Words in the brain's language. *Behavioral and Brain Science, 22*, 253–279, discussion 280–336.

Pulvermüller, F. (2001). Brain reflections of words and their meaning. *Trends in Cognitive Science, 5*, 517–524.

Pulvermüller, F. (2005). Brain mechanisms linking language and action. *Nature Review Neuroscience, 6*, 576–582.

Pulvermüller, F., Shtyrov, Y., & Ilmoniemi, R. (2005). Brain signatures of meaning access in action word recognition. *Journal of Cognitive Neuroscience, 17*, 884–892.

Pylyshyn, Z. W. (1984). Computation and cognition. MIT Press.

Raposo, A., Moss, H. E., Stamatakis, E. A., & Tyler, L. K. (2009). Modulation of motor and premotor cortices by actions, action words and action sentences. *Neuropsychologia, 47*, 388–396. doi:10.1016/j.neuropsychologia.2008.09.017.

Rüschemeyer, S. A., Brass, M., & Friederici, A. D. (2007). Comprehending prehending: Neural correlates of processing verbs with motor stems. *Journal of Cognitive Neuroscience, 19*, 855–865.

Rüschemeyer, S. A., Lindemann, O., van Elk, M., & Bekkering, H. (2008). Embodied cognition: The interplay between automatic resonance and selection-for-action mechanisms. *European Journal of Social Psychology*, *39*, 1180–1187.

Rüschemeyer, S. A., Lindemann, O., van Rooij, D., van Dam, W., & Bekkering, H. (2010). Effects of intentional motor actions on embodied language processing. *Experimental Psychology*, *57*, 260–266.

Sato, M., Mengarelli, M., Riggio, L., Gallese, V., & Buccino, G. (2008). Task related modulation of the motor system during language processing. *Brain and Language*, *105*, 83–90.

Shtyrov, Y., Hauk, O., & Pulvermüller, F. (2004). Distributed neuronal networks for encoding category-specific semantic information: The mismatch negativity to action words. *European Journal of Neuroscience*, *19*, 1083–1092.

Simmons, W. K., Hamann, S. B., Harenski, C. L., Hu, X. P., & Barsalou, L. W. (2008). fMRI evidence for word association and situated simulation in conceptual processing. *Journal of Physiology Paris*, *102*, 106–119. doi:10.1016/j.jphysparis.2008.03.014.

Smith, E. E., & Medin, D. L. (1981). *Categories and concepts*. Harvard University Press.

Solomon, K. O., & Barsalou, L. W. (2004). Perceptual simulation in property verification. *Memory and Cognition*, *32*, 244–259.

Tettamanti, M., Buccino, G., Saccuman, M. C., Gallese, V., Danna, M., & Scifo, P., et al. (2005). Listening to action-related sentences activates fronto-parietal motor circuits. *Journal of Cognitive Neuroscience*, *17*, 273–281.

Tettamanti, M., Manenti, R., Della Rosa, P. A., Falini, A., Perani, D., & Cappa, S. F., et al. (2008). Negation in the brain: Modulating action representations. *Neuroimage*, *43*, 358–367. doi:10.1016/j.neuroimage.

Tulving, E. (1972). Episodic and semantic memory. In: E. Tulving, & W. Donaldson (Eds.), Organization and memory (pp. 381–403). Academic Press.

van Dam, W. O., Rüschemeyer, S. A., & Bekkering, H. (2010). How specifically are action verbs represented in the neural motor system: An fMRI study. *Neuroimage*, *53*, 1318–1325. doi:10.1016/j.neuroimage.2010.06.071.

van Dam, W. O., Rüschemeyer, S. A., Lindemann, O., & Bekkering, H. (2010). Context effects in embodied lexical–semantic processing. *Frontiers in Psychology*, *1*, 150. doi:10.3389/fpsyg.2010.00150.

van Dam, W. O., van Dongen, E. V., Bekkering, H., & Rüschemeyer, S. A. (2012). Context-dependent changes in functional connectivity of auditory cortices during the perception of object words. *Journal of Cognitive Neuroscience*, *24*, 2108–2119. doi:10.1162/jocn_a_00264.

van Elk, M., van Schie, H. T., & Bekkering, H. (2008). Semantics in action: An electrophysiological study on the use of semantic knowledge for action. *Journal of Physiology*, *102*, 95–100. doi:10.1016/j.jphysparis.2008.03.011.

van Elk, M., van Schie, H. T., Zwaan, R. A., & Bekkering, H. (2010). The functional role of motor activation in language processing: Motor cortical oscillations support lexical–semantic retrieval. *Neuroimage*, *50*, 665–677. doi:10.1016/j.neuroimage.2009.12.123.

Williams, L. E., & Bargh, J. A. (2008). Experiencing physical warmth promotes interpersonal warmth. *Science*, *322*, 606–607.

Willems, R. M., Toni, I., Hagoort, P., & Casasanto, D. (2010). Neural dissociations between action verb understanding and motor imagery. *Journal of Cognitive Neuroscience*, *22*, 2387–2400. doi:10.1162/jocn.2009.21386.

Yeh, W., & Barsalou, L. W. (2006). The situated nature of concepts. *American Journal of Psychology*, *119*, 349–384.

www.ingramcontent.com/pod-product-compliance
Lightning Source LLC
Chambersburg PA
CBHW071418290426
44108CB00014B/1885